The Key Strategies That Can Make Anyone a Successful Leader

Be the Leader Everyone Wants to Follow

Zohra Sarwari

D0907652

Eman Publishing
P.O. Box 404
FISHERS, IN 46038
USA

www.emanpublishing.com

Order Online: www.zohrasarwari.com

ISBN 13: 978-0-9841275-0-4
ISBN 10: 0-9841275-0-X
LCCN: 2009938277

EMAN
publishing

Cover Design by Zeeshan Shaikh

Printed in the United States of America

2

The Key Strategies That Can Make Anyone a Successful Leader

Be the Leader Everyone Wants to Follow

Zohra Sarwari

Dedication

'(Our Lord! Accept this from us; You are the All-Hearing, the All-Knowing).'

(The Qur'aan: Chapter 2, Verse 127)

Acknowledgments

In the name of Allaah, the Most Gracious, the Most Magnificent. All praise is due to Allaah, Lord of the universe. We praise Him, and seek His help and His forgiveness, and we seek His protection from the accursed Satan. Whomever Allaah guides will never be misguided, and whomever He allows to be misguided will never be guided. I bear witness that there is no deity worthy of worship except Allaah, who is One; alone, and has no partners. I bear witness that Muhammad is His servant and messenger; may the blessings of Allaah be upon him, his family, his companions, and the righteous that follow them until the Day of Judgment.

I would like to thank my family and friends for all their support, especially Zeeshan, Madeeha, and Saqib Shaikh, who are an asset to my team *masha'Allaah*. A very special thanks goes to Dr. Daoud Nassimi for all of his efforts and hard work in reviewing the Islamic information and references of this book – *jazaakum Allaahu khayran*! May Allaah (SWT) reward you all - *aameen*!

Terminology

1. **"ALLAAH"** is the Arabic name for 'THE ONE SUPREME UNIVERSAL GOD'.
2. **"SWT"** is an abbreviation of the Arabic words **"Subhaanahu wa Ta'aalaa"** that mean **"Glory Be To Him."**
3. **Al-Qur'aan:** The Book of Allaah. A divine guidance for mankind. The FINAL TESTAMENT.
4. **Muslim** is one who has submitted to the Will of ALLAAH.
5. **PBUH** means Peace be upon him.
6. **PBUT** means Peace be upon them.
7. **Alhamdulillaah** means 'Praise is for God!'
8. **5 Daily Prayers: 1. Fajr** (pre-dawn): This prayer starts off the day with the remembrance of Allaah (SWT); it is performed before sunrise. **2. Dhuhr** (noon): After the day's work has begun, one breaks shortly after noon to again remember Allaah (SWT) and seek His guidance. **3. 'Asr** (afternoon): In the late afternoon, people are usually busy wrapping up the day's work, getting kids home from school, etc. It is an important time to take a few minutes to remember Allaah (SWT) and the greater meaning of our lives. **4. Maghrib** (sunset): Just after the sun goes down, Muslims remember Allaah (SWT) again as the day begins to come to a close. **5. 'Isha** (evening): Before retiring for the night, Muslims again take time to remember Allaah's (SWT) Presence, Guidance, Mercy, and Forgiveness.
9. **Du'aa** is supplication in Islam.
10. **Insha'Allaah** means 'if Allaah wills'.
11. **Hadeeth** means the actions and sayings of Prophet Muhammad (PBUH), reported by his companions and collected by scholars who came after them in books.
12. **Jannah** means Paradise.

13. **Masha'Allaah** means "It is what Allaah willed.'
14. **Halaal** means anything that is permissible under Islamic law.
15. **Sunnah** means the deeds, sayings and approvals of Muhammad (PBUH).
16. **Sahaabah** means Companions of the Prophet Muhammad (PBUH).
17. **Deen** means Religion.
18. **(RA)** stands for *Radiya 'Llaahu 'anhu,* which means "May Allaah be pleased with him."
19. **Surah** means a chapter in Qur'aan.
20. **Aakhirah** means 'The Hereafter' or the life of the next world
21. **Muslimah** is the word used for a Muslim woman.
22. **Hijrah** means emigration.

Table of Contents

Strategy #1

Purpose

By

Zohra Sarwari

"Without a Purpose in Life, You're not really Living a Life."
Zohra Sarwari

This quality is vital to become a leader, because if you don't have a purpose-driven life, a reason to move forward, you will not do it. Only when you have a purpose will you look beyond the problems, beyond the lack of knowledge in that area, lack of experience in that area, and push your way in, *insha'Allaah*.

The dictionary defines **_purpose_** as: '*The object towards which one strives or for which something exists; an aim or a goal*'. Every great leader must have a purpose, and their purpose must be bigger than all of the obstacles they face. I will give you an example of a true story that I once witnessed:

A woman was in a really bad car accident and the doctors told her that she would not be able to walk; they told her that that was a fact of life. She however, told herself that she will walk again; she hated being in a wheelchair; she hated depending on others; she knew that if she tried her best, *insha'Allaah* she would walk again. Well within 2 years, I believe she walked again *masha'Allaah*.

Her life was filled with many obstacles; she had lost her mother at the tender age of 3 or 4; she was living on the streets at the age of 14; to name but a few. Anyway, to cut a long story short, she was once again involved in a car accident, and this time the doctors told her that her legs were gone; that she never fully recovered from the first accident, that there was no chance of her ever walking again, and that she should just accept it. Well, this woman refused to accept it; however first of all she wanted to be financially secure, so she worked on her business from home until she was financially independent. Once this goal was achieved, she decided that she would walk again; she had made up her mind, and she was going to give it her best. It took her 2 years of working with a physical therapist, a lot of pain, and hours of tears, but she did it; *masha'Allaah* she was able to walk again. Her story is one that I have never forgotten; no matter how difficult it was for her, she made up her mind and went for it, because she refused to accept what the doctors told her.

Now I want all of you to think with me for a minute; what would you do if you found out that you could never walk again? What would you do if you found out that you had to depend on governmental aid because you couldn't work due to your handicap? All of the cases that I have witnessed; most people have accepted their fate and not fought it.

Of course everything is in the Hands of Allaah (SWT); however, we have been given a free will to try. We are given a free will to do our best, and then let Him take care of the rest, yet most of us accept what others have decided for us, and don't even try to do anything about it.

Prophet Muhammad (PBUH) said,
"Every illness has a cure, and when the proper cure is applied to the disease, it ends it, Allaah Willing."
(Muslim)

Think about this Hadeeth; how powerful is it? Every illness has a cure, and this is exactly what this woman thought; she didn't just accept the doctor's decision, she fought to figure out the cure. Yet most of us accept the solution given to us, instead of fighting to see if we can find a more amicable solution. In the end the results are up to Allaah (SWT), not us, but if we don't try, how will we know what the results might be?

More than anything, this woman had a purpose in life; she wanted to be someone, she wanted to do her best and have no regrets. She wanted to show that it can happen. This is what it means to have a purpose in life. Do you have that? Do you have this strong desire to do your best no matter what obstacles come in your way? Do you have the motivation to keep going when the going gets tough? Do you have that burning flame inside you; that you won't give up on your mission until the day you die? This is what it means to have a purpose in life.

This quality is one that helps differentiate between the leaders and the followers. We are all followers of the Prophets (PBUT), as we take them as role models to help us to understand Allaah's (SWT) Message; but are we leading others in the same manner? We have seen many great leaders in history, so what's stopping us? The answer is a simple fact that we don't have a purpose in life. *Insha'Allaah* in this chapter I will be discussing more examples of people with a purpose in life, and how you too can have a purpose in your life, *bi idhnillaah*.

My first example of great leadership and purpose is the best example from all of mankind; it is the example of a man whose life changed at the age of 40, when Allaah (SWT) sent down the Angel Jibreel (AS) to give him the message of Islaam. This is the greatest man who has ever lived; this is **Prophet Muhammad (PBUH)**. What was his purpose?

Prophet Muhammad (PBUH) was truly purpose-driven in his life. For the first 40 years of his life, he lived a life free from the worship of idols, but his life was lived more or less like anyone else in his time. However, when the message of Allaah (SWT) started coming to him (PBUH), his purpose-driven life began.

It was then that no matter how severe the torture, how cruel the people were, how difficult it was to meet with the Muslims to teach them, he still did it. He (PBUH) had a message, and he had to answer to Allaah (SWT), which meant he had to do this. There were no choices, he was sent as the final messenger to all of mankind. He was the seal of the Prophets. Talk about purpose-driven life, *masha'Allaah!* What is amazing is that as you are reading about his life, you begin to realize that had he not had a purpose in his life, he would have given up after all of the obstacles that he faced. This is how important having a purpose in life is.

There are many examples in Prophet Muhammad's (PBUH) life that show this trait of having a purpose, and I encourage all of you to read his biography to see for yourself. *Insha'Allaah* in this chapter we will go through only one of the biggest tests in his life to see if he would give up his purpose or not; when his uncle, Abu Talib was approached by the Quraysh, and Muhammad (PBUH) was asked by him what he wanted in return for giving up this message that there is only One God.

The leaders of the Quraysh had offered Prophet Muhammad (PBUH) everything; from women to being the King of Arabia, just as long as he would give up calling to Islaam; give up on the notion that there was only One God.

Imagine being told that you would get everything that you could desire just to give up this notion of there being only One God; many people would jump for this chance. They would give up their souls for wealth, women, status, and power. However, this is the true test of life, to see if one is fulfilling their mission, or has some other intention in mind. Yet, the Prophet Muhammad (PBUH) did not give up his mission in relaying the message to the people to worship only One God, *masha'Allaah*.

Step 1:

How can YOU find your purpose in life?

These are the questions everyone should ask themselves:
- Am I passionate about anything?
- Is there anything that I love doing even if I didn't get paid for it?
- Is there a cause that I would fight for because it is right?

These are questions you need to ask yourself, and also remember, as Muslims we need to make sure our actions and intentions are according to what Allaah (SWT) has ordered us. So before you get started on your passion or mission in life, you should ask a trustworthy Islamic scholar, if what you wish to do is *halaal* or not, and if not he will provide you with evidence indicating why it isn't *insha'Allaah*.

Step 2:

Write down your **MISSION** in life.

Step 3:

Check your intentions:

- Why are you doing this?
- What is your intention?
- Is it for fame?
- Is it for money?
- Is it for power?

Ask yourself about your intention, and please keep in mind this *hadeeth* when you are checking your intentions:

"All actions are judged by motives, and each person will be rewarded according to their intention. Thus, he whose migration was to God and His Messenger, his migration is to God and His Messenger; but he whose migration was for some worldly thing he might gain, or for a wife he might marry, his migration is to that for which he migrated."
(Saheeh Al-Bukhari & Saheeh Muslim)

Step 4:

Write out your goals:

Make a goal sheet; have the end in mind, but then start from the bottom which is the idea, and write small steps to accomplish the goals, *insha'Allaah*.

Note that the end we should have in mind is the *aakhirah*, and the end result we should all be working for is to gain entry into

Jannah, insha'Allaah. How will this goal or dream that you have helped achieve that *insha'Allaah*?

Step 5:

Be patient:

As easy as this may seem, please remember that you need to be patient, and take each step as something big; there will be hundreds of little steps that will be added before the big steps take into effect, *insha'Allaah.* For example, one wants to be a bestseller; first they must write the book, and then publish it, then market it so much that *insha'Allaah* it becomes a bestseller.

Step 6:

Never quit!

Even though times will get tough, and how you envisioned your 'purpose' is different to the reality, don't worry. If this happens, check your intentions, and see if they are the same as they were when you began this project. Make sure you're always on track with your intentions *insha'Allaah.*

Insha'Allaah, this should be enough to help you start living a PURPOSEFUL life.

Lessons from an Oyster
-Anonymous

There once was an oyster
Whose story I tell,
Who found that some sand
Had got into his shell.

It was only a grain,
but it gave him great pain,
For oysters have feelings
Although they're so plain.

Now, did he berate
the harsh workings of fate
That had brought him
To such a deplorable state?

Did he curse at the government,
Cry for election,
And claim that the sea should
Have given him protection?

'No', he said to himself
As he lay on a shell,
'Since I cannot remove it,
I shall try to improve it'.

Now the years have rolled around,
As the years always do,
And he came to his ultimate
Destiny stew.

And the small grain of sand
That had bothered him so
Was a beautiful pearl
All richly aglow.

Now the tale has a moral,
for isn't it grand
What an oyster can do
With a morsel of sand?

What couldn't we do
If we'd only begin
With some of the things
That get under our skin.

The Emperor's Seed
-Anonymous

An emperor in the Far East was growing old and knew it was time to choose his successor. Instead of choosing one of his assistants or his children, he decided something different. He called young people in the kingdom together one day. He said, *"It is time for me to step down and choose the next emperor. I have decided to choose one of you."*

The kids were shocked! But the Emperor continued. *"I am going to give each one of you a seed today; one very special seed. I want you to plant the seed, water it and come back here one year from today with what you have grown from this one seed. I will then judge the plants that you bring, and the one I choose will be the next emperor!"*

One boy named Ling was there that day and he, like the others, received a seed. He went home and excitedly told his mother the story. She helped him get a pot and planting soil, and he planted the seed and watered it carefully.

Every day he would water it and watch to see if it had grown. After about 3 weeks, some of the other youths began to talk about their seeds and the plants that were beginning to grow. Ling kept checking his seed, but nothing ever grew.

3 weeks, 4 weeks, 5 weeks went by; still nothing!

By now, others were talking about their plants but Ling didn't have a plant, and he felt like a failure. 6 months went by; still nothing in Ling's pot. He just knew he had killed his seed. Everyone else had trees and tall plants, but he had nothing.

Ling didn't say anything to his friends; he just kept waiting for his seed to grow. A year finally went by and all the youths of the kingdom brought their plants to the Emperor for inspection.

Ling told his mother that he wasn't going to take an empty pot but his mother said he must be honest about what happened. Ling felt sick to his stomach, but he knew his mother was right.

He took his empty pot to the palace. When Ling arrived, he was amazed at the variety of plants grown by the other youths. They were beautiful; in all shapes and sizes. Ling put his empty pot on the floor and many of the other kids laughed at him. A few felt sorry for him and just said, *"Hey, nice try."*

When the Emperor arrived, he surveyed the room and greeted the young people. Ling just tried to hide in the back. "*My, what great plants, trees and flowers you have grown,"* said the Emperor. *"Today, one of you will be appointed as the next emperor!"*

All of a sudden, the Emperor spotted Ling at the back of the room with his empty pot. He ordered his guards to bring him to the front. Ling was terrified, *"The Emperor knows I'm a failure! Maybe he will have me killed!"*

When Ling got to the front, the Emperor asked his name. *"My name is Ling,"* he replied. All the kids were laughing and making fun of him. The Emperor asked everyone to quiet down.

He looked at Ling, and then announced to the crowd, *"Behold your new emperor! His name is Ling!"* Ling couldn't believe it. Ling couldn't even grow his seed; how could he be the new emperor?

Then the Emperor said, *"One year ago today, I gave everyone here a seed. I told you to take the seed, plant it, water it, and bring it back to me today. But I gave you all boiled seeds, which would not grow. All of you, except Ling, have brought me trees, plants and flowers. When you found that the seed would not grow, you substituted another seed for the one I gave you. Ling was the only one with the courage and honesty to bring me a pot with my seed in it. Therefore, he is the one who will be the new emperor!"*

If you plant <u>honesty</u>, you will reap trust.
If you plant <u>goodness</u>, you will reap friends.
If you plant <u>humility</u>, you will reap greatness.
If you plant <u>perseverance</u>, you will reap victory.
If you plant <u>consideration</u>, you will reap harmony.
If you plant <u>hard work</u>, you will reap success.

If you plant <u>forgiveness</u>, you will reap reconciliation.
If you plant <u>openness</u>, you will reap intimacy.
If you plant <u>patience</u>, you will reap improvements.
If you plant <u>faith</u>, you will reap miracles.

But:

If you plant <u>dishonesty</u>, you will reap distrust.
If you plant <u>selfishness</u>, you will reap loneliness.
If you plant <u>pride</u>, you will reap destruction.
If you plant <u>envy</u>, you will reap trouble.
If you plant <u>laziness</u>, you will reap stagnation.
If you plant <u>bitterness</u>, you will reap isolation.
If you plant <u>greed</u>, you will reap loss.
If you plant <u>gossip</u>, you will reap enemies.
If you plant <u>worries</u>, you will reap wrinkles.
If you plant <u>sin</u>, you will reap guilt.

So be careful what you plant now; it will determine what you will reap tomorrow. The seeds you scatter now will make life worse, or better your life or the ones who will come after. Yes, someday, you will enjoy the fruits, or you will pay for the choices you plant today.

Activities

I want you to ask yourself and answer these four powerful questions:

1. *Am I 100% happy with myself?*

_____

_____

_____

_____

_____

_____

2. *What would it take for me to be 100% happy with me?*

_____

_____

_____

_____

_____

_____

3. *If there is one thing that I would love to do - whether I got paid for it or not - what would it be?*

_____

_____

_____

_____

_____

_____

4. *Will Allaah (SWT) be happy with this mission and passion that I have?*

_____

_____

_____

_____

_____

_____

I Will Do More
- Anonymous

I am only one, but I am one.
I cannot do everything, but I can do something.
And what I can do, I ought to do.
And what I ought to do, by the Grace of Allaah,
I will do.
I will do more than belong ... I will participate.
I will do more than care ... I will help.
I will do more than believe ... I will practice.
I will do more than be fair ... I will be kind.
I will do more than dream ... I will work.
I will do more than teach ... I will inspire.
I will do more than earn ... I will enrich.
I will do more than give ... I will serve.
I will do more than live ... I will grow.
I will do more than talk ... I will act.
I will be more than good ... I will be good for something.

Author's Biography

 **Zohra Sarwari**

Zohra Sarwari is an established author, coach, entrepreneur, publisher and international speaker. As a public speaker and Muslim life coach, Zohra focuses on helping people achieve their goals and working with individuals on resolving specific challenges within their lives.

Zohra Sarwari has a Bachelors Degree in Psychology, a Masters Degree in Business Administration and is currently working on a Bachelor's Degree in Islamic Studies. Zohra is currently home schooling her own children, as well as teaching and training others about business and entrepreneurship. Zohra has been interviewed and featured on TV, radio, magazines, and newspapers all around the world *masha'Allaah.*

Author of 10 Books:

She is the author of 10 books; **"9 Steps To Achieve Your Destiny"** is her first published book. This book explores the steps that, if practiced daily, will change your life.

Her other books are, **"Imagine that Today is YOUR Last Day"**, **"NO! I AM NOT A TERRORIST"**, **"Are Muslim Women Oppressed?"**, **"Powerful Time-Management Skills For Muslims"**, **"Speaking Skills Every Muslim Must Know"**, **"Who Am I?"** and she has also co-authored this book, **"The Key Strategies That Can Make Anyone A Successful Leader"**, and lastly **"How To Raise A Successful Kidpreneur"** *insha'Allaah.* As well as this she has also written 2 e-books, **"Time-Management For Success"** and **"Become a Professional Speaker Today"**, over 40 videos, and many articles.

Strategy #2

Motivation

By

Rukhsana Hanjra

"Having motivation is the path to achieving success. Having the attributes of the role model-leader is the way forward. Having the vision to be successful and helping others to success is worthy of contentment. Feeling the passion for change is the fuel for the fire. So, what are you waiting for? Because time is borrowed; let's hold on to the rope of Allaah (SWT) and make a difference in someone's life."
Rukhsana Hanjra

Are you the person who leads people, or are you the person who wants to be led? So which one are you; the driver, or the passenger?

If you are the passenger and wish to become the driver, how can you achieve this? Simple! Make clear decisions, know where you want to go and strive to reach your destination.

What Is Motivation?

Motivation is the driving force which comes from within oneself, which then leads to action in the behaviour. So, for example, if you wanted to lose weight because it was going to make you feel good, the internal drive is "feeling good" about yourself, which is followed by the action to change the diet and start to exercise. It is this burning desire that achieves fulfilling results. This is what motivation can do; it can take you from being a passenger in the back seat, to the driver in the front seat; who has control and direction. Understanding and applying the principles of motivation can accelerate learning, improve performance, increase perseverance, and overcome obstacles.

People often lose motivation because of three factors;

- Lack of confidence
- Lack of direction
- Lack of focus

This is clearly visible in people who do not have a focus, make misjudgements and then lose confidence in them and begin to lose motivation. To turn motivation into performance is a challenge; however, this is affected by the individual's capacity and willingness to perform. In Islaam, the Qur'aan and Sunnah have examples of the clarification of intention (motivation), which is the direct result of a deliberate decision and conscious effort to achieve a specific goal.

On the authority of Umar Ibn Al-Khattab, who said, I heard the Messenger of Allaah (PBUH) say:
"Deeds are only by intentions, and every man shall have only what he intended."
(Bukhari and Muslim)

This is why motivation is a vehicle to success as intentions are the driving force behind achieving motivation.

Highly motivated individuals are people who have clarity of vision and objectives, and self-confidence. They feel the need for responsibility and control. They have the desire to take risks, accepting correction or criticism, and need for recognition, just like the driver. These characteristics are not in-born but can be cultivated and nurtured in any individual.

<u>Islaamic Perspective of Motivation</u>

Motivation in Islaam is based on *Eemaan*, *Taqwaa* and *Tawbah*.

Eemaan (Faith) as a Motivator:

Motivation is mentioned many times directly or indirectly in the Qur'aan. *Eemaan* forms the basis and is the energizing force for all motivations. *Eemaan*, according to Sayyid Maudoodi is the seed and Islaam is the fruition. Inner faith and practice are tightly coupled with one another and are interdependent. The essential components of this motive are the strong unshakable belief in Allaah, the Eternal, the Absolute, the Creator of the universe; and the strong unshakable belief in the fact that man will be held accountable for his deeds in this life.

Taqwaa as a Motivator:

Taqwaa is having consciousness and fear of Allaah. Consciousness of Allah keeps a Muslim alert about Allah's presence in offering the needed support and in watching how one is spending his/her time, etc. The motivation of fear is the human emotion that enables man to either avoid danger and problematic situations or face or resolve them.

Tawbah (Repentance) as a Motivator:

The concept of *tawbah* comprises another very important type of motivation, for without repentance a person can stay on a wrong path which would direct him to committing harm to himself rather than directing his efforts towards good deeds.

Reward and Punishment:

Reward and punishment as a doctrine in the Qur'aan is fundamentally different from that found in other religions. Muslims are encouraged to act out of both fear and hope, striking a fine balance between the two; fear of Allaah's Punishment, and hope in His (SWT) Mercy.

Building upon the foundation of Islaamic concepts of motivation; this can lead a person to achieve attributes of leadership. Some of the attributes that leaders need vary from being kind and compassionate to: honesty, competence, being forward-looking, providing inspiration, strength of character, humility, kindness, modesty and simplicity, and taking responsibility for others.

The best person is one who is able to combine all the above qualities and know where and when to use them. He/she is also able to bring out the best qualities in others. Being a good or bad leader, whether in the home or community, plays a major role in the development of that home or community; it can either make it more functional or it can become dysfunctional and create an unhappy environment.

An example of this can be seen in the home where both parents can hold very clear roles for their families using the above qualities of leadership so that there are clear boundaries and responsibilities; thus both parents would serve as very strong role models for the children as well as society at large. For this reason the attributes of leadership are very important as they are not just inspirational for that person, but also for others around them. This is very significant as it has a ripple effect like that of the waves in the sea.

This is how motivation develops when leaders/parents or anyone in a position of leadership/management shows the "Obedience" and "Willingness" to work in unity or as a team, as emphasized in the Qur'aan and the *seerah* of the Prophet Muhammad (PBUH).

In particular this can be seen in the community, when a community leader is willing to adapt and understand the communities' needs, the community becomes united under the obedience of the community leader. This in return motivates the community to develop and progress. The community can be successful when positive change is taking place and motivation levels begin to rise. This can also be applied in the home; if the leader/manager is addressing the needs of his/her family by communicating effectively, willingness to understand, being a role model of good governance according to the Islaamic guidelines, then everyone under him/her will be obedient; they will be willing to be part of the team, creating a highly motivating environment and thus becoming a successful family.

The example of Prophet Muhammad (PBUH) emphasizes a major role of the Muslim leader: to protect his community against tyranny and oppression, to encourage God-consciousness and *taqwaa*, and to promote justice:

Ibn 'Umar (May Allaah be pleased with them) reported that the Messenger of Allaah (PBUH) said,
"All of you are guardians and are responsible for your subjects. The ruler is a guardian and is responsible for his subjects; the man is a guardian of his family; the woman is a guardian in her husband's

house and responsible for her wards; a servant is a guardian of his
master's property and responsible for his ward. So all of you are
guardians and are responsible for your subjects".
(Al-Bukhari and Muslim)

A leader or manager needs to be humble, and must never let his or her ego get the better of him/her. In fact, the Qur'aan describes true servants of Allah in general as:

"Those who walk on the earth with humility."
(The Qur'aan, 25:63)

What Can Motivation Achieve?

Motivation can lead to achieving the desirable results. It can lift someone's confidence levels from the bottom of the ladder to the top of the ladder. By aiming for higher goals this can bring the abilities and skills of the individual to the best; a person can become a fulfilled individual. An example of such a person is Helen Keller.

Helen Keller was born in Alabama on June 27, 1880. She contracted an illness at the age of 19 months, described by the doctors as "an acute congestion of the stomach and the brain." This left her deaf and blind.

Helen Keller had chosen to take the path to success and made a difference for the millions of disabled people in the world, and not just for herself. She showed that disability need not be the end of the world.

Helen Keller's parents took her to see a specialist in ENT (Ear, nose and throat) for advice. The doctor referred them to the

'Perkins Institute for the Blind'. The director of the school asked former student Anne Sullivan, who was herself visually impaired and then only 20 years old, to become Keller's instructor *(Wikipedia)*.

Anne immediately started to teach Helen how to finger spell. Helen could repeat these finger movements but could not understand their meaning. At the same time, Anne was finding it difficult to help her to understand, and she was also finding it difficult to control Helen's bad behavior. Anne moved into a small cottage on the land of the main house with Helen, so that she could help Helen improve her behavior. Anne was dealing with Helen's table manners as she was eating with her hands and also from everyone's plates.

Anne really worked hard to make a difference to Helen's table manners and taught her how to brush her own hair and wear her shoes; this however led to more and more tantrums. The way Anne dealt with these tantrums was by refusing to "talk" to Helen by spelling words on her hands.

With time, Helen's behaviour began to change and they became closer to each other. Soon, after a month of Anne teaching, a feeling of a miracle took place.

Anne led Helen to the water pump, and everything changed; while Anne poured the water over Helen's hand, she spelt out the word 'water' in Helen's other hand. This became a method of association for Helen; Anne could see from Helen's face that she understood.

Straightaway Helen asked Anne for the name of the pump to be spelt on her hand, and then she carried on asking the names of everything she touched, including Anne's name. Anne spelt the word "Teacher" on Helen's hand. In the next few hours Helen learnt the spelling of thirty new words.

Helen's progress was amazing, because her ability to learn was never seen in anyone who was blind/deaf. Anne then began teaching Helen to read with Braille. The school director was very eager to give Helen a high profile, so he wrote articles about Helen which led to a great deal of public interest.

Helen Keller had achieved success by not only learning English but French, German, Greek and Latin. She also became an author, political activist and a lecturer.

In Helen's own words, *"The public must learn that the blind man is neither genius nor a freak nor an idiot. He has a mind that can be educated, a hand which can be trained, ambition which it is right for him to strive to realize, and it is the duty of the public to help him make the best of himself so that he can win light through work"* **(Wikipedia.org).**

What leadership characteristics did Helen Keller have? What did she achieve in her life?

How can someone who is without sight and without hearing make a difference to millions of people? What made Helen Keller so motivated? Can you answer this question and explain in the context of the Islaamic perspective on motivation.

_____

_____

_____

_____

_____

How Motivation Can Be Achieved?

Motivation can be achieved by having a belief in you; a belief which matches who you really are and what you can really achieve. Do you know yourself? If not, then discover the important you. Have a vision; a vision of success and achievements. In that vision there are no obstacles, if it feels there are, then look to the opposite side and find ways of removing them, and don't allow them to stop you from conquering them. Conquer them before they conquer you!

Thoughts become much clearer and you no longer suffer from mental constipation (mental blockages). When all the negative trash has been thrown in the bin, your thoughts become crystal clear. The thoughts of success just flow and flow, just like a clear river running into the sea. Just feel how big you can become, just by believing in yourself as Zara, the tree did:

Zara: The Tree

Zara was a tree, a tree that was trying very hard to grow but could not find its direction. Its growth was determined by others; her thoughts were controlled by the sun (parents), moon (siblings) and stars (peers and environment). The tree was not getting much of the sun; it was never warm; the moon never shone its light on her, and the stars were scattered and would only be seen from time to time. So Zara - the tree just did not look very nourished and did not have healthy roots. The branches were always wavering; the leaves were dry and discolored, and the tree did not stand out. It searched for the love and care of others, but it was never given it. She wanted the nourishment and waited for the fertilizer to be given to help its growth. It waited and waited for passers-by to give it a glance, but everyone ignored it, as if it was of no importance. Zara - the tree lost all its confidence and felt worthless.

Zara - the tree began questioning her worth and all her expectations of others towards her. Her thoughts would trail to 'Buts'… 'Ifs'… 'How is it possible…?' Surely, the purpose was for everyone to take care of Zara - the tree. She was neglected, ignored and was of little importance.

Perhaps we all go through life expecting others to take care of us, and waiting most of our life for something to happen, and before we know it, half or more of our life has passed us by; and who said time waits for us? No, I am afraid to say, time does not wait. Al-Hasan Al-Basree said, *"Oh son of Adam! You are nothing but a number of days, whenever a day passes then part of you has gone."*

Furthermore, nothing can emphasize this point more beautifully than **Surah Al-Asr (103:1-3):**

"By the time, verily man is in loss, except those who believe and do righteous good deeds, and recommend one another to the truth, and recommend one another to patience."

This was a reminder for Zara - the tree, that time was precious and every day was a valuable day. With this attitude of expectations from others, Zara - the tree had fallen into a cycle of sadness and disappointment; trying to work out why she was not receiving what she needed. But do we know what we really need? Helen Keller said that, *"Character cannot be developed in ease and quiet. Only through experience of trial and suffering is the soul strengthened, ambition inspired, and success achieved"* **(Wikipedia.org).**

So the importance of self-analysis is valuable in order to have the ability to recognize our strengths and our weaknesses.

Abu Bakr (RA) understood the importance of knowing and understanding himself, as well as the feedback from others. Upon the occasion of his first *khutbah* as Caliph, he stated: '*O people! I have been selected as your trustee although I am no better than anyone of you. If I am right, obey me; if I am misguided, set me right*' **(Rafi Ahmed Fidai; The concise history of the Muslim world p. 68).**

Ali ibn Abi Talib (May Allaah (SWT) be pleased with him) said, "*One who knows himself, knows his Creator*" **(Ghulam Sarwar: Islam, Beliefs and Teachings).**

If we do not reflect and try to understand ourselves better and acknowledge our strengths and weaknesses, like Abu Bakr (RA) did, how can we be righteous and just to ourselves and to others? We fall into the risk of becoming like a loop that goes round and round and cannot break the cycle. So we become just like a rigid tree that is hard and narrow and shows limited thoughts and beliefs; which leads us to having no flexibility. How many of us have fallen into this trap? So what are we waiting for? What did Zara - the tree do? Read on!

Imagine if you stopped waiting for everyone around you to give you the attention, time, love, support and recognition! What would it feel like? Maybe you would feel lonely; maybe you would feel empty, or maybe you would feel at a loose end? Then, what if Zara - the tree offered you an alternative? *INSTEAD*, switch the light bulb on! Can you feel the brightness; clarity; even a clearer path? And thus your journey begins as Zara's did. It leads her to connecting with her Creator and having *eemaan*. The tree itself became the symbol of *eemaan*; a tree that takes in carbon dioxide and gives out oxygen; without it there would be no life (spirituality).

A tree holds such a multitude of benefits; from providing us with ripe fruits, delicious produce, constant food, shelter to continual goodness (*eemaan*). So the tree of *eemaan* will always benefit you. *Eemaan* benefits you by providing you with complete stability; where the roots of the tree are well established (rooted) or grounded. Zara -

the tree did not shake with the wind again or get blown away but *INSTEAD* ... do you know what happened?

Have a sense of purpose of who you are and where you are going, just like Zara - the tree did; once the light bulb was switched on and the light of guidance began. From then on the tree began growing; it grew tall and strong; it became sturdy, providing shelter, comfort and beauty for itself and for everyone who stood and admired her. So a tree of *eemaan* had been planted; a tree that could only grow taller and taller and aim for *Jannah*. Around the bottom of the tree were beautiful flowers that were growing and giving beauty and freshness; they were Zara's grandchildren, playing around the tree and enjoying every moment of each new day.

Zara - the tree no longer needed to wait for others to appreciate and love her because Zara - the tree had an abundance of love, so much so that whoever came close to her had a share of it too. Zara - the tree became the most admired tree that everyone wanted to know about.

"Many persons have the wrong idea of what constitutes true happiness. It is not attained through self-gratification but through fidelity to a worthy purpose."
(Helen Keller)

"See you not how Allaah sets forth a parable? A goodly word as a goodly tree, whose root is firmly fixed, and its branches (reach) to the sky. Giving its fruits at all times, by the Permission of its Lord, and Allaah sets forth parables for mankind in order that they may remember."
(Surah Ibraaheem, 14:24-25)

Zara - the tree was motivated because she stopped looking outwards and began to look inwards; others did not matter anymore except to give what she could and share what she had. The energy was spent on discovering herself, and not others. In other words, 'Where focus goes energy flows'. Levels of motivation began to rise when gratitude took the place of self-pity. When she started counting all the blessings she had and not counting what she did not have.

When life had a purpose and meaning, and time was valuable, then there was no stopping her. The end of the earth would not be further enough. It was constantly climbing new hills and she never turned back to look at the pitfalls. How motivation paves the way to success and contentment! It is a choice we can make; it depends on the road you take; it's the journey you are looking for, and it's the goal you want to achieve.

Success and rewards are all yours! You just need to help yourself; just like Zara - the tree did; just as Helen Keller did, and especially how the greatest role model of all times, Prophet Muhammad (PBUH), and his Companions did. Take the lead and become the leader; the driver and not the passenger.

Can you answer the following questions? be honest! Otherwise you are only bluffing yourself and no one else ...

- How motivated am I?

- What will I need to do to achieve my goals?

- Why have I not started? Afraid of the challenge? Still holding on to your fears?

- Is it going to be action or excuses?

Make a choice! Become motivated!

'Allaah is the Light of the heavens and the earth;
The parable of His Light is as (if there were) a niche
and within it a lamp: the lamp is in a glass, the glass as it were a
brilliant star,
lit from a Blessed Tree,
an olive, neither of the east nor of the west,
whose oil would almost glow forth (of itself),
though no fire touched it.
Light upon Light!
Allaah guides to His Light whom He wills.
And Allaah sets forth parables for mankind,
and Allaah is All-Knower of everything.
In houses (mosques) which Allaah has ordered to be raised,
in them His Name is remembered.
Therein glorify Him in the mornings
and in the afternoons or the evenings,
Men whom neither trade nor sale
diverts from the remembrance of Allaah
nor from performing the prayer
nor from giving the Zakaat. They fear a day
when hearts and eyes will be overturned.
That Allaah may reward them
according to the best of their deeds,
and add even more for them out of His Grace.
And Allaah provides without measure to whom He wills.'
(Surah An-Noor, 24: 35-38)

Author's Biography

 Rukhsana Hanjra

Rukhsana is married and has three grown-up children. Rukhsana came to England from Pakistan in 1969 when she was 7 years old. She has lived in South-London for 40 years. She resumed her studies as a mature student whilst raising her three young children. She successfully completed her BSc in Psychology from Surrey University, and an MSc in Developmental Psychology from the Institute of Education.

She then went on to train as a counsellor and concurrently set up a community centre called the 'Islamic Resource Centre', which provides a free counselling, advice and support service. Rukhsana has worked in the community for nearly 10 years, dealing with issues of depression, lack of confidence, breakdown of relationships, domestic violence, child abuse, personality disorders and family mediation. The centre has become a registered charity and today there are over 25 volunteers who dedicate their energies by giving up their free time and skills for the benefit of the community. May Allaah (SWT) reward all of them and accept their work - *aameen*!

Whilst managing the centre Rukhsana trained as a lecturer and taught Psychology at Kingston College. More recently Rukhsana has become a certified life coach, trained by Muhammad Alshareef. At present, Rukhsana is in the process of completing Cognitive Behavioural Therapy training.

For further information on life coaching visit me at visit Muslimahcoach.com or email Rukhsana info@muslimahcoach.com or Rukhsana@muslimahcoach.com.

Acknowledgments:

I would like to say *'jazaaki Allaahu khayr'* to Zohra Sarwari for initiating this book and to her team for all their efforts. Zohra has been a source of inspiration and I wish her all the success in this world and the hereafter.

I would like to thank my husband Khalid for his support, my children; Aisha and her husband, Abid; Faisal and his wife, Sanah; and Bilal, for believing in me. Not to forget my two grandsons, Aadam and Omer, who add beauty to every new day.

Finally, thank you to my parents who worked very hard in raising me. May Allaah (SWT) ease their old age and bring them all the peace, comfort and joy in their lives - *aameen*.

Strategy #3

Confidence

By

Henna Ahmed

"Du'aa can do miracles; always put your hands up in du'aa".
Henna Ahmed

The topic 'Confidence' has been chosen to discuss and write about to help you get a better insight of this quality. There are many reasons for choosing this quality but namely the reason behind it is an inspiration by a person of my age who possessed this quality and shone like a bright light, in not only my life but in hundreds of people's lives. I was fortunate enough to be around this person, later became a close friend, and until this day we are still friends, *masha'Allaah*.

Amber - My Inspiration!

Now *alhamdulillaah* (all praises belong to Allaah) that I have spent many years in her company; she's awesome, inspiring and so funny; I could go on and on about her qualities, and Allaah knows best. She is simply one of the best Muslimahs I've met. Although religion wasn't her main concern, she had strong values and I felt them emanating from her. She wasn't afraid to take risks, nor join in and talk with people. Most importantly she was very influential and fearless.

Meeting Amber for the First Time:

So back in year 7, Amber was friends with many people from many backgrounds, namely English. She is a British-Pakistani like me and was held in high esteem by her peers, who supported her all the way from year 7 to year 11. Can you imagine in this day and age when racism and nationalism is rife that this person being a British-Pakistani could influence and be part of people who were white?

Argument between Amber and My Friends:

One day at Rothens High School, a couple of months into year 9, Amber was hanging around with her friends during the break. When my friends and I saw her with a group of white girls; some of my friends had a problem with her hanging around with them. My friends started calling her names such as 'tart', 'dirt-bag' and even 'lesbian'. I don't know where this came from; I couldn't believe they were saying all this. I tried to tell them to back off but that didn't help.

I was fearful of the consequences. You see this was their level of respect for other races. This should definitely not be the case because then we forget that we're all human. Eventually my friends got bored and walked away laughing. I felt upset and felt this kind of behavior was unjustified; it wasn't right. Just imagine how Amber and her friends felt.

Later during lunchtime, whilst my friends and I sat eating our lunch and just chilling; the same group of girls from break time was sat at the opposite end of the canteen from us. They were looking angry and pointing at us. At this point we realized that something was going to happen. Towards the end of lunchtime they came over to us and surrounded our table; I mean surrounded us like a swarm of bees.

Finally the Situation Settled Down:

They were too many to count; at this point we were scared; we didn't expect to face these consequences. The girls started arguing with two or three of my friends who they recognized were involved. Now my friends were making lame arguments and couldn't justify what they had done. I've got to say that these girls; Amber's friends were pretty confident; they stood up for themselves. They didn't allow my friends to treat them like dirt or let anyone belittle them. That's how they got their point across. They were civilized to my friends by talking to them instead of using their fists.

After seeing my friends struggle (it being their own fault) I spoke up, but some of the girls told me to stay out of it. I wanted to apologize to them, to clear things up between them, but my friends eventually did. The girls put them in their place and after that my friends were weary of those girls.

We had learnt a lot from that confrontation, and my friends didn't get away with it but I guess what happened was for the better. Something brilliant was coming our way, and it happened at the end of the year; Amber became one of our friends! Yeah sure we had formed our group of friends and we were going to be rivals with another group of girls in our year, but that's a whole new chapter.

Start of Our Friendship:

I tell you that this was the start of a beautiful friendship. She was so confident; not arrogant but down-to-earth, realistic and positive. This is where I have to bring in this beautifully inspiring quote:

'Our deepest fear is not that we are inadequate. Our deepest fear is that we are powerful beyond measure. It is our light, not our darkness that most frightens us. We ask ourselves, 'Who am I to be brilliant, gorgeous, talented, fabulous?' Actually, who are you not to be? Your playing small does not serve the world. There is nothing enlightened about shrinking so that other people won't feel insecure around you. We are all meant to shine, as children do. And as we let our own light shine, we unconsciously give other people permission to do the same. As we are liberated from our own fear, our presence automatically liberates others.'
"Our Deepest Fear" by Marianne Williamson, quoted by Nelson Mandela in his 1994 Inaugural Speech.

Recapturing My Dreams:

I never understood the above until now, when I was almost giving up on my dreams but *Alhamdulillaah* (all praise belongs to God) I had people who told me to keep trying. Now I've met Sister Zohra Sarwari who has given me this chance to be a co-author with her; WOW!

Also now that I've finished high school, and Amber and I have gone to different colleges is when I realized how much she meant to me.

Amber's Influence:

Well back to this beautiful friendship; someone who was a leader in my life. Amber was a person who I followed and respected and so did so many others. By the time we were in year 10, she and I became very good friends. Everything about her amazed me, from her reactions to situations (they were spot on) to the ability to make friends within a matter of minutes, *masha'Allaah*. Eventually she had the whole school talking to her, most of whom were very good friends with her. She may not know that but I witnessed her unique abilities every day of my life at high school with her. Now see what I'm talking about; a truly remarkable individual who I admire with all of my heart and soul.

We spent many happy and sad times together, shared the laughter and supported one another when times were tough. It's amazing what one person with confidence, high self-esteem, individuality, strong values and respect for all people can do for society. She also made friends with majority of the teachers; yes with teachers! She made people smile, and feel good about themselves, and she was assertive; as she wouldn't do anything that went against her values; she was firm and could stand her ground.

I strongly believe that this quality is vital, especially for the Muslim community because we need to be positive examples;

representatives of Islaam. Now you may have had to understand Islaam the hard way, you get what I mean, through the tears, nasty comments, beatings etc; me too.

However, you and I both know that Islaam is not responsible for these unjustified means of teaching. We know Islaam is so much more than this. *Insha'Allaah* (God-Willing) we have to embrace the opportunity to change the way we do things and how we follow Islaam, as the new generation; and that's by following the Qur'aan and the Sunnah (teachings of the Prophet (PBUH)).

Moreover, it's a way of life, we are told that our intentions (the inside part of us) are just as important as our actions. So we have to improve our intentions, and after that we can focus on acting positively. Good words and actions go hand in hand.

Remember also that,

"The deeds most loved by Allaah [are those] done regularly, even if they are few."
(Bukhari)

'Those to whom the people said, "Verily, the people have gathered against you, therefore fear them." But it only increased them in faith, and they said: Allaah is sufficient for us, and He is the Best Disposer of affairs."
(Surah Aali 'Imraan, 3:173)

The above is very powerful to me; look at what they were told but that only reaffirmed their faith. WOW! *SubhaanAllaah*! We definitely have got to strive for this quality.

Now, let us look at the best man who ever walked the earth; Prophet Muhammad (PBUH) *(Muhammad No.1 'The 100, a*

Ranking of the Most Influential Persons in History' by Michael H. Hart).

"Muhammad (PBUH) was forty when, during one of his many retreats to Mount Hira for meditation, during the month of Ramadaan, he received the **first revelation** from the Archangel Jibreel (Gabriel). On this first appearance, Jibreel (AS) said to Muhammad (PBUH): "Iqra'", meaning 'Read' or 'Recite'.

Muhammad replied, "**I cannot read**", as he had not received any formal education and did not know how to read or write.

The Angel Jibreel (AS) then embraced him until he reached the limit of his endurance and after releasing him said: *"Iqra'"*. Muhammad's (PBUH) answer was the same as before. Jibreel (AS) repeated the embrace for the third time, asked him to repeat after him and said these words, which are recorded as the first five verses of **Surah 96** in the Qur'aan:

"Recite in the name of your Lord who created! He created man from that which clings. Recite; and thy Lord is most Bountiful, He who has taught by the pen, taught man what he knew not."

Thus it was in the year 610 CE the revelation began.

Muhammad (PBUH) was terrified by the whole **experience of the revelation** and fled the cave of Mount Hira *(Qur'aan, 81:19-29).* When he reached his home, tired and frightened, he said to his wife to cover him in a blanket. After his awe had somewhat abated, his wife Khadijah (RA) asked him about the reason of his great anxiety and fear. She then assured him by saying: *"Allaah (The One God) will not let you down because you are kind to relatives, you speak only the truth, you help the poor, the orphan and the needy, and you are an honest man."* Khadijah (RA) then consulted with her cousin Waraqa, who was an old man, possessing knowledge of previous revelations and scriptures.

Waraqa confirmed to her that the visitor was none other than the Angel Jibreel (AS) who had come to Moosa (AS). He then added that **Muhammad (PBUH) is the expected Prophet. Khadijah (RA)** accepted the revelation as truth and was the first person to accept Islaam. She supported her husband in every hardship, most notably during the three-year 'boycott' of the Prophet's (PBUH) clan by the pagans, the Quraysh. She died at the age of sixty-five in the month of Ramadaan soon after the lifting of the boycott in 620 CE.

This example shows how much confidence Khadija (R.A) had in Allaah (SWT) and Prophet Muhammad (SAAW).

Jibreel (AS) continued to visit the Prophet (PBUH) as commanded by Allaah revealing Ayaat (verses) in Arabic over a period of twenty-three years. The revelations that he received were sometimes a few verses, a part of a chapter or the whole chapter. Some of the revelations came down in response to an inquiry by others (Muslims and non-Muslims). The revealed verses were recorded on a variety of available materials (leather, palm leaves, bark, shoulder bones of animals), memorized as soon as they were revealed, and were recited in daily prayers by Muslims.

Per Allah's order, Jibreel (AS) also visited the Prophet (PBUH) throughout his mission, informing and teaching him of events and strategy as needed to help in the completion of the prophetic mission. The Prophet's (PBUH) sayings, actions, and approvals are recorded separately in collections known as Hadeeth." For more information about a brief biography of Prophet Muhammad (PBUH), visit the following website: *http://ipaki.com/content/html/26/383.html*.

Confidence of the Sahaabah (RA)

Also another great man, who was also a *sahaabah* (Companion), Abu Bakr As-Sideeq (RA) showed such confidence when he said; *"Muslims can never be defeated because of small numbers. But if their sins (bad deeds) overwhelm them, they will meet defeat. So let you all keep away from sins of all kinds". (Sahaba.net).* This was said to the Muslim army, when the commanders asked his permission to merge together, as Abu Bakr (RA) had split the army up into 4 battalions, for they were very small in number. This battle was against Byzantium who sent four huge armies, which were several times more numerous than the Muslim army; however this great man's (RA) faith never wavered, instead he used this as an opportunity to become better from inside; truly remarkable.

I'd like to say to you all that please read, feel and visualize along with me whilst I tell you the story at the beginning, as I wrote it, I felt it flowing and coming out of me. Also don't forget how much I love you all (my brothers and sisters in Islaam and humanity) for the sake of Allaah (SWT). Also if you get anything out of this chapter please contemplate on, "Our Deepest Fear" by Marianne Williamson, as that sums up the whole topic of my chapter.

Remember that I took initiative to get involved with this project which was offered to anyone and everyone by Sister Zohra Sarwari. Moreover, I even got stuck on what I was going to write, but in the end after a couple of days of stressing out, I realized I needed to ask Allaah (SWT) for help. I made *du'aa* (supplication), which lasted a couple of minutes, and I asked Allaah (SWT) for help; and it's amazing how immediately straight after I became so passionate to write about what I did. We can do it; I know we are in a bizarre time when people are very far from religion and other people in general (time of disconnectedness); crime rates are high so are alcohol, drugs and all sorts of other things, but never forget that we have to leave this world behind one day; we are only travelers.

Also I would love to be a mirror for you as that's what we are meant to be for one another; so that we can try and stay righteous and good-willed, as said by the Prophet (PBUH). Lastly, I wanted to leave a story for the ending, hope you like it.

Confidence and Self-Esteem
-Anonymous

'Confidence' and 'Self-Esteem' were best friends; they went everywhere together. If Confidence bought a new dress, Self-Esteem bought one just like it. They were very close. One day a new kid came to their school; his name was 'Peer Pressure'. He had a friend called 'Hateful Words'.

They decided to give Confidence a hard time; they constantly teased her. They forced her to do terrible things. It was so terrible that Confidence lost Self-Esteem. When Self-Esteem wanted to start some classes, Confidence said they wouldn't be any good.

Then one day, Peer Pressure introduced Confidence to Doubt; he wanted to ruin Confidence, but Peer Pressure said he couldn't yet. Self-Esteem couldn't understand what was wrong with Confidence. Confidence now hung around with 'Depression', 'Low Self-Esteem' and 'Overeating'. These girls were friends of Peer Pressure. Self-Esteem no longer had any friends. She no longer felt good about herself. She went to see her pastor.

'Pastor Good Words' told her how to talk to Confidence. He introduced her to his daughter, 'Encouragement'.

Encouragement and Self-Esteem went to find Confidence. Self-Esteem hoped she wasn't too late. The girls found Confidence in a stupor; she was no longer a vibrant, happy, young girl. There were dark circles under her eyes. She had gained so much weight from eating that she couldn't move. Encouragement gasped and Self-Esteem cried. Self-Esteem begged Encouragement to do something.

Encouragement began to hug Confidence. She kissed her and loved her. She told her that she was a beautiful young lady who had a lot going for her. Encouragement held Confidence so tightly that Self-Esteem thought she would smother her. Confidence began to cry. As she cried, she seemed to lose weight. Then a bright light suddenly glowed from Confidence and she began to smile.

Peer Pressure and his friends didn't like what Encouragement was doing and tried to attack her. They hit her and pulled at her, but they couldn't pull her away from Confidence, *"Get away from me, Peer Pressure. Take your friends and go. You no longer have any power over me"*. Confidence was now a glowing light. She and her friends made sure that Peer Pressure and his gang never bothered anyone in their town again.

'If you feel that Encouragement is not your friend, then try to find Encouragement in yourself. Self-Esteem and Confidence will follow'.
(http://asoa.maldivesinfo.com/2005/09/19/confidence-and-self-esteem/)

Build Self-Confidence

1. Dress Decently:

Be humble in your dress code. Wear clean and covered clothes that follow within the guidelines of Islaam. Many people think that you must dress fashionably to feel good, but really your feeling good is from within not by what you wear alone. Many people have this misconception that they must wear the best fashions to feel good, but I say that you must feel good first, and then anything that you wear *insha'Allaah* will shine on you.

2. Walk Energetically:

Sometimes the way a person walks is the easiest way to know if that person is confident or not. Those people who are confident usually walk straight and energetically, compared to those who have low self-confidence. So this means that just your way of walking could show it all; that whether you are confident about yourself or about what you are doing or not. You can easily make yourself look confident by walking actively. You will feel the difference in your confidence levels *insha'Allaah*.

3. Good Body Language:

Another important aspect for building confidence is your body language. Your body language could show your feelings, state of mind and confidence levels. Let's suppose if you walk with drooped shoulders, a low head and slowly, it could show that you are not confident.

It could also show your lack of interest in your duties or tasks you are to achieve. If you look unhappy or tired, this may show boredom. Give your posture a total transformation; improve your way of sitting, standing and making direct eye contact. Good body language leaves a good impression of your personality on whoever you meet.

4. Personal Motivation:

Personal motivation is a self-help approach of gaining confidence using different methods. If motivational speakers are available in your area, you can go and listen to their speeches and attend their seminars or classes. But if this is not possible, then you can boost your self-confidence yourself. All you have to do is to use the good old technique of making a speech about any topic; let's say about your strengths and weaknesses in front of a mirror, repeat it in your head or in front of a group of family members or friends. Just giving 30 minutes to yourself will *insha'Allaah* help you feel the changes deep inside.

5. Be Thankful:

Always think positive. This way you will always look at your strengths and not your weaknesses and ultimately you will feel confident about yourself. Make it a habit on focusing on the bright side of the picture when you have to keenly observe any situation from both perspectives. Keeping an eye on the bright side makes you thankful for everything you have been granted and you feel contented instead of being thankless all the time.

We should be thankful for everything we have; it may be our health, relationships, successes, achievements or even for our every breath we are taking, instead of always complaining about the things we don't have.

Allaah is the All-Knower; so if we don't have something there must be a reason. If you thank Allaah in every condition whether you get what you want or you don't, I am sure you will feel more satisfied and confident *insha'Allaah*.

6. Appreciate Other People:

Feelings of jealousy and hatred not only damage our personality but our impression on others, people start disliking us as a person. So the action and reaction philosophy applies throughout our life. The way we behave we get the same in return from others. So it means if we will be polite in turn others would want to behave the same way with us. Our approach towards people is the way they will perceive us.

The way we approach people, is the way they perceive us. If we start considering ourselves superior to others, talk low of them, use destructive criticism, highlight the negatives or weaknesses of people, making fun of them and gossiping we will leave a bad impression.

Adopt the habit of appreciating the efforts of people even if they are minor and give everyone respect. Ultimately you will feel the change in yourself as well as your popularity amongst people around you *insha'Allaah*.

7. Don't Be A Back Bencher:

People are mostly afraid of sitting in front while they are in a classroom, college events, office meetings, presentations etc. This is because they lack confidence so they prefer taking the back seats. Instead the approach should be to always try to get the front seats so that you can easily understand the person presenting or giving a lecture. Sitting in front is very beneficial, you will not only be prominent and get noticed but you will understand more and while doing that you will gain confidence about yourself *insha'Allaah*.

8. Speak Your Mind:

Malik narrated that Prophet Muhammad(SAW) said, *"Who believes in Allâh and the Last Day should talk what is good or keep quiet. (i.e. abstain from dirty and evil talk, and should think before uttering)."*
(Bukhâri 8/157)

Don't hesitate in expressing your opinion. Don't fear that maybe you are wrong at least you should express it so you will gain confidence. You mostly see a display of hesitation or expressing opinions during group discussions. People have points to make but they don't speak out because they fear rejection or being considered stupid. Remember at such times everyone is in the same boat and everyone is ready to listen other's opinion. So be expressive and speak out your mind.

This will not only boost your confidence but also make others realize the importance of your opinion and how intelligent you are.

9. Physical Fitness:

A powerful personality is a combination of mental and physical fitness. When you spend time on making your appearance look appealing, you should also spend time on maintaining good health and physical fitness as well.

Physical fitness is essential for your mental fitness. And if you are physically fit you will realize that you will automatically feel confident about yourself. So if you want to be confident and look confident pay attention to your physical fitness as it strengthens your mind as well.

10. Focus:

Focus is another important aspect of building confidence. Sometimes, people give unnecessary importance to their looks, appearance, personality etc. but ignore their performance. This shows their real focus has got diverted to things which don't need extra attention and while doing that you are ignoring the aspects which require your real focus. It depends all on your focus and your decision of which things need how much focus, so always give equal importance to every aspect instead of focusing on just a few aspects.

Focus more on your successes, accomplishments and your role for the good of society and humanity as a whole, you will automatically feel more satisfied and confident. So always prove yourself to be a productive element; this will help you in achieving success and gaining recognition.

"Each time we face our fear, we gain strength, courage, and confidence in the doing."
Anonymous

Activities

Write down **10 Things** you will do to build your self-confidence *insha'Allaah*:

1. _____
   _____

2. _____
   _____

3. _____
   _____

4. _____
   _____

5. _____
   _____

6. _____
   _____

7. _____
   _____

8. _____
   _____

9. _____
   _____

10. _____
    _____

Author's Biography

 **Henna Ahmed**

"I am 17 years old and live in the UK. Currently I'm in College, I hope to keep studying thus furthering my knowledge to become a more active and productive member of society and a much more conscientious Muslimah." Henna is the eldest child in her family and has seven siblings.

In her free time Henna loves engaging in many kinds of sports and keeping fit. She also tries to take part in different activities in her community. For more information on Henna please visit her website, www.hennaahmed.com.

Acknowledgments

I would like to thank my mom and dad as without their sacrifices none of this would have been possible, and the same goes for Sister Zohra Sarwari; who has been so helpful, reliable and absolutely fantastic. Thank you all! May Allaah grant you the best in both worlds - *aameen*!

Strategy #4

Patience

By

Khadija Begum

*"It is through patience that one can truly **achieve their dreams.**"*
Khadija Begum

In order for you to become the person that everyone wants to follow, you must develop and practice patience in your daily life. Patience is a very important characteristic of a leader; without this quality you can never truly become successful in anything. As a leader you will have to face many challenges to achieve your dreams; it is in those difficult times that you will need patience.

<u>Meaning of Patience</u>

So what does 'patience' mean? *"Patience is the capacity for calmly enduring difficult situations"*,
(http://www.thefreedictionary.com/patience).

A person who acts patiently is capable of restraining himself from doing acts that are displeasing to Allaah, and continues to do what is righteous.

Leaders who practice patience are capable of calmly waiting for an outcome or result; they are not hasty or impulsive to reach their goals. If things do not go the way they have planned, they don't beat themselves up about it; they know the difference between things that they are able to control and the things they have no control or influence over. A wise leader would spend most of their time and attention on things that they are able to control; they let go of things which they have no control over since they realize any time spent on these is ineffective and wasteful.

George-Louis de Buffon once wrote, *"Genius is nothing but a great aptitude for patience."*

Patience is a characteristic that can be developed; however it is not an easy task. Those who do practice patience are rewarded in many ways. We should practice patience in our lives just like we use other skills.

Here are three things you can do instantly:

1. Try to see the big picture.
2. Refocus your mind on other more important things.
3. Avoid inappropriate comparisons.

Islaam's Perspective on Patience

Patience is considered a weapon for the believer; to use when difficulties and troubles become an obstruction. Patience and its related terms have been mentioned in the Qur'aan more than 90 times. It has also been mentioned in many *ahadeeth*. All of the Messengers of Allaah suffered great hardships in their lives, but they remained patient; always thanking Allaah for His many blessings, and avoided complaining. As a consequence of their patience and their confidence in Allah, Allaah removed their hardships and promised them great rewards in the hereafter.

Types of Patience

The **three most common types** of patience, which not only develop a strong personality, but also produce a sense of thankfulness for all the blessings one has compared to what one doesn't have are:

1. Patience in abstaining from sin.
2. Patience in persevering in the good (i.e., obeying Allaah, etc).
3. Patience during calamities and disasters.

Patience makes a person realize that hardships and prosperity are a part of life and we should be facing them both with strength and character, instead of becoming thankless. In Islaam, patience is one of the greatest and most precious virtues of life. As a Muslim, we believe that through patience we become closer to Allaah *subhaanahu wa ta'aalaa*. No other manner is mentioned as often as patience.

In the Qur'aan Allaah (SWT) orders us to seek help through patience and *salaah*. He says,

"Seek help in patience and As-Salaat (the prayer). Truly, Allaah is with As-Sabireen (the patient)."
(Surah Baqarah, 2:153)

I can certainly say that we all want Allaah to be with us all the time, for He is the One who takes care of us regardless of our situation; and Allaah says in the Qur'aan that He is with the people who are patient. So if you want Allaah to be with you, why not be patient?

There are several verses in the Qur'aan where Allaah commands us to the kind of characteristics we should acquire in our roles as Muslim leaders. He chose the qualities of a leader in Islaam to be one who has both patience and certainty in one's *deen*:

"And We made from among them, leaders, giving guidance under Our command, when they were patient and used to believe with certainty in Our Ayat."
(Surah As-Sajdah, 32:24)

In this verse Allaah is clearly stating that leadership that is rightly guided by Allaah will come with two things; patience and complete trust in Allaah *(SWT)*.

Patience is something that is very easy to understand, but sometimes it is extremely difficult to implement if our *eemaan* is not strong. When a leader practices patience, it means that he can stop himself from despairing and panicking when he is faced with trials. The believers' true patience, however, is very different from mere endurance. They are aware that Allaah creates whatever happens to them for a reason and that therefore it contains some hidden benefit. Knowing that Allaah has determined the best possible destiny for them, they meet everything that is outside of their control with pleasure and an open heart. Allaah explains the attitude of the faithful who would end up to Jannah in the following verse:

"Those who are steadfast and put their trust in their Lord."
(Surah al-'Ankaboot, 29:59)

A true leader would also be able to withhold himself from too much complaining to people about his misfortune. Our attitude should be just like Yaqoob (AS) when he said:

"I only complain of my grief and sorrow to Allaah, and I know from Allaah that which you know not."
(Surah Yoosuf, 12:86)

As a leader, we need to learn to mainly complain to Allaah (SWT) since there is great benefit in this; while on the other hand complaining to people will rarely bring us any benefit since most of the time, they will not be able to do anything to improve our circumstances. However, if we complain to Allaah He has all the power to do whatever He may please. Complaining to Allaah is actually a form of true patience and will be rewarded tremendously, while complaining to people could be the opposite.

Allaah wants the leaders to be patient during difficult times; however, He doesn't just want us to have patience, rather he wants beautiful patience from the believers as He says:

"So be patient, with a beautiful patience."
(Surah al-Ma'aarij, 70:5)

So what is beautiful patience? Beautiful patience means that you are patient without having any fear or anxiety of what the future holds for you; you are content with what Allaah has bestowed upon you. No matter what hardships you face, you recognize that such hardships are a test from Allaah.

You continue to worship Allaah without uttering any words that will be displeasing to Him. Basically, beautiful patience is patience with contentment, not just with your tongue but with your heart as well. It is true that in those painful moments, our heart will ache and the eyes may tear, after all we are human; however, our heart should not be in a state of rejection or giving up, but rather it should be in a state of patience.

Beautiful patience is also a positive patience; for example, someone could be in a very abusive relationship and they want to live in a peaceful household, but they are not taking the necessary means to get out of that current situation. In this case, we would not say that this is beautiful patience. Beautiful patience means that you are being patient and you are making an effort to improve your condition; this would be considered beautiful patience. It is not beautiful patience when you are just sitting around and saying, *"I am being patient"*.

Everything in life requires patience; from raising a child to overcoming calamity. If we analyze our lives we can conclude that most of the problems that we encounter are due to our lack of patience. For example, people who commit fornication do not have the patience to wait until marriage, or those who cheat on exams are just too lazy to study. Perfecting our *deen* and our lives are all related to patience.

Sayings of Prophet Muhammad (PBUH) on Patience

There are many sayings of the Prophet, Muhammad (PBUH) on patience.

It has been narrated by Abu Moosaa al-Ash'ari (RA) who said the Messenger of Allaah (PBUH) said:
"Patience is Light."
(Sahih Muslim)

The Prophet (PBUH) described patience as light because the calamities and troubles that come in our lives are like darkness, and patience is the light that helps us overcome this darkness.

Prophet (PBUH) said,
"Whosoever would be patient, Allaah will give him patience, and no one is granted a gift better and more comprehensive than patience".
(Al-Bukhari and Muslim)

So don't think about the worldly gifts you possess; the best gift that you can possibly have is that of having patience.

The Prophet (PBUH) also said,
"Be mindful of Allaah, you will find Him before you. Get to know Allaah in prosperity and He will know you in adversity. Know that

what has passed you by was not going to befall you; and that what has befallen you was not going to pass you by. And know that victory comes with patience, relief with affliction, and ease with hardship."
(Tirmidhi)

Another beautiful saying of the Prophet, Muhammad (PBUH) is,

"The matter of the believer is amazing. All of his matters in his life are good, and this is only applicable to the believer. If a calamity befalls him, he is patient, and this is a good thing for him. If he receives a bounty, he thanks Allaah, and this is a good thing for him."
(Muslim)

Abu Sa`id and Abu Hurayrah (May Allaah be pleased with them) reported that the Prophet (PBUH) said,
"Never a believer is stricken with a discomfort, an illness, an anxiety, a grief or mental worry or even the pricking of a thorn but Allaah will expiate his sins on account of his patience."
(Bukhari & Muslim)

Abu Sa'id Al-Khudri (May Allaah be pleased with him) reported that: 'Certain people of the Ansaar asked the Messenger of Allaah (PBUH) for monetary help and he gave them; then they again asked him and he gave them until all what he possessed was exhausted.

Abu Yahya Suhaib b. Sinan said that Prophet Muhammad(PBUH) said, *"Wondrous are the believer's affairs. For him there is good in all his affairs, and this is so only for the believer. When something pleasing happens to him, he is grateful, and that is good for him; and*

when something displeasing happens to him, he is enduring (sabar),
and that is good for him. "
(Muslim)

Patience of
Prophet Muhammad (PBUH)

During the Makkan period, in the early days of the Message, when the Prophet (PBUH) would proceed outside and invite the people towards Allaah in order to embrace Islaam, he would be severely tortured and persecuted, but he always observed patience. One of these instances is that of an old woman who had a habit of throwing rubbish on Prophet Muhammad (PBUH) whenever he passed by her house! Muhammad (PBUH) had to pass that house daily on the way to the mosque. Even when the old woman threw rubbish on him he would pass by silently, without showing any anger or annoyance. This was a regular daily event.

One day when the Prophet (PBUH) was passing by, the woman was not there to throw the rubbish. He stopped, and asked the neighbor about her well-being; wondering why she wasn't dropping any rubbish on him. The neighbor informed the Prophet (PBUH) that the woman was sick and bedridden. The Prophet (PBUH) politely asked permission to visit the woman.

When allowed, he entered the house; the woman thought that he had come to take his revenge as she was unable to defend herself due to the sickness. But the Prophet (PBUH) assured her that he had come to her, not to take any revenge, but to see her and to look after her needs, as it was the command of Allaah that if anyone is sick, a Muslim should visit him and should help him if his help is needed.

The old woman was greatly moved by this kindness and love of the Prophet, Muhammad (PBUH); she understood that he was truly the Prophet of Allaah, and Islaam was the true religion. She accepted Islaam at once, *masha'Allaah*. It is because Muhammad (PBUH) was patient with this woman that she ended up embracing Islaam.

Abu Bakr (RA):
The Scorpion Sting!

"Another incident where we see how patience is being practiced is during the *Hijrah* of the Prophet (PBUH) with Abu Bakr (RA), in the cave of Thawr. The Prophet (PBUH) fell asleep on the lap of Abu Bakr (RA), whilst Abu Bakr (RA) had his legs stretched to cover the holes in the walls; fearing something would come out of one of them and sting the Prophet. So Abu Bakr got stung by a scorpion, and he did not scream or move because he did not want to disturb the Prophet's (PBUH) sleep, until the tears fell from his eyes on the Prophet (PBUH), and woke him up." *(Sahaba.net)*

Therefore, we should try hard to practice patience in our lives, and we should know that we can all gain patience with practice and struggle. If we successfully achieve this goal our life will become easier, and we will become more thankful.

The Butterfly
-Anonymous

A man found a cocoon of a butterfly. One day a small opening appeared. He sat and watched the butterfly for several hours as it struggled to force its body through that little hole. Then it seemed to stop making any progress; it appeared as if it had gotten as far as it could, and it could go no further. So the man decided to help the butterfly; he took a pair of scissors and snipped off the remaining bit of the cocoon.

The butterfly then emerged easily; but it had a swollen body and small, shriveled wings.

The man continued to watch the butterfly, because he expected that, at any moment, the wings would enlarge and expand to be able to support the body, which would contract in time.

Neither happened! In fact, the butterfly spent the rest of its life crawling around with a swollen body and shriveled wings. It was never able to fly.

What the man, in his kindness and haste, did not understand was that the restricting cocoon and the struggle required for the butterfly to get through the tiny opening were God's way of forcing fluid from the body of the butterfly into its wings; so that it would be ready for flight once it achieved its freedom from the cocoon.

Sometimes struggles are exactly what we need in our lives. If God allowed us to go through our lives without any obstacles, it would cripple us.

We would not be as strong as what we could have been. We could never fly!

Patience Is a Sign of Inner Peace
-Anonymous

Patience is a sign of inner peace,
Acceptance of the gift of life and death.
Though time may toll the passing of each breath,
In time one takes the measure of one's lease.
Each moment holds its small infinity,
Neither more nor less than that of years.
Clouds can tear down mountains with their tears,
Even as winds churn the changeless sea.

Author's Biography

 **Khadija Begum**

Khadija Begum was born in the city of Chittagong, Bangladesh and moved to United States when she was eight. She graduated from Overbrook Regional High School as a "Graduating Junior" with NJ Star scholarship.

Currently she is a student at Rutgers, The State University of New Jersey. In 2006, she was honored with membership in the National Society of High School Scholars.

She is also an active member of Muslim *Ummah* of North America (MUNA); a *da'wah* and social organization which provides many services to the Muslim and non-Muslim community of North America. She holds the position of secretary of MUNA Youth Women Sub-Chapter in South Jersey. Additionally, she is a member of MUNA Youth Women National Leadership Program, which has the vision of producing MUNA's future leaders. Besides working with the youth, Khadija also works with the children in her community. She is the coordinator of MUNA Children department in South Jersey.

Presently she also coordinates and teaches at Muslim American Community Association (MACA) Summer School.

In 2008, she was trained as a life coach by Shaykh Muhammad AlShareef. For more information on life coaching email Khadija at: khadija@khadijabegum.com.

Strategy #5

Creativity

By

Alya Nuri

"Being creative means you can fail, but remember after you fail you will succeed insha'Allaah."
Alya Nuri

Creative Touch

"On the first day as President Abraham Lincoln entered to give his inaugural address, just in the middle, one man stood up. He was a rich aristocrat. He said, 'Mr. Lincoln, you should not forget that your father used to make shoes for my family.' And the whole senate laughed; they thought they had made a fool of Abraham Lincoln. But Lincoln - and that type of people are made of totally different mettle; Lincoln looked at the man and said, 'Sir, I know that my father used to make shoes in your house for your family, and there will be many others here because the way he had; nobody else can. He was a creator. His shoes were not just shoes; he poured his whole soul in it. I want to just ask you, have you any complaint? I can make another pair of shoes. But as far as I know nobody has ever complained about my father's shoes. He was a genius, a great creator and I am proud of my father.'

The whole senate was struck dumb. They could not understand what kind of man Abraham Lincoln was. He had made shoe making an art, creativity, and he was proud because his father did the job so well that not even a single complaint had ever been made. It does not matter what you do. What matters is how you do it - of your own accord, with your own vision, with your own love; then whatever you touch becomes gold." (http://www.squidoo.com/abelincolnshoes)

This quality is very important in leaders, because all leaders need to be creative and think of different solutions, and alternate ways of doing things. Being creative is thinking outside the box. For example, the Prophet, Muhammad (PBUH) in the Battle of Khandaq (The Trench), as usual was listening to the advice of the different *Sahaabah* (RA), and it was Salmaan Al-Farsi (RA) who gave the suggestion to make a trench; which Prophet Muhammad (PBUH) accepted. If the Prophet Muhammad (PBUH) was not open-minded and creative in asking for advice then they might have lost the battle.

In the Qur'aan, Allaah (SWT) tells us to think about the creation,

'Verily! In the creation of the heavens and the earth, and in the alternation of night and day, there are indeed signs for men of understanding. Those who remember Allâh (always, and in prayers) standing, sitting, and lying down on their sides, and think deeply about the creation of the heavens and the earth, (saying): "Our Lord! You have not created (all) this without purpose, glory to You! (Exalted are You above all that they associate with You as partners). Give us salvation from the torment of the Fire.'
(Surah Aali-'Imraan, 3:190-191)

In Islaam we must be creative to create new things. This is how Algebra was born; this is how the number zero was created by Muslims.

'Clean out a corner of your mind and creativity will instantly fill it.'
Dee Hock

'Creativity can be described as letting go of certainties.'
Gail Sheehy

A great example of creativity is that of Thomas Edison who invented the light bulb; but by being creative what else did we make? Flashlights, key lights, book lights, etc.

Prophet Muhammad (PBUH) showed this attribute of creativity in battles; planning, learning, and hiding.

The Battle of the Trench
(Al-Khandaq)

"The Battle of the Trench (Al-Khandaq), or, of the Clans (Al-Ahzaab) *(Ibn Hisham, Vol. II, p. 214)*, as it is sometimes called, took place in the month of Shawwaal, 5 AH. Such armed discord was fought with great difficulties, and overcome with comparable courage.

When the Prophet (peace be upon him) learned of the Jews' evil designs to wipe the Muslims out of existence, he conferred with his companions (May Allaah be pleased with them) on how to deal with the threat. It was decided that they would launch a defensive war, resisting the attack of the enemy against the city, instead of facing the coalition in a pitched battle outside Madeenah. So the Prophet (peace be upon him) assembled a force of three thousand armed men in defense of the city.

A Persian companion called Salmaan (may Allaah be pleased with him), advised digging a trench along the side of Madeenah which was laid open to cavalry attack *(Ibn Hisham, Vol. pp. 224)*. This technique was well-known to the Iranians. Salmaan is reported to have said: *'Prophet of God, when we feared a charge by the cavalry we used to dig trenches to keep the invaders at bay'.*

The Prophet (peace be upon him) agreed to his suggestion and decided to have a trench dug in the open ground, lying to the north of Madeenah. The city was exposed to assault only on that side and was well protected to the west, south and east by clumped plantations, volcanic rocky plains and granite hills; presenting a considerable obstacle to the cause of a mounted army.

The Prophet (peace be upon him) marked the planned ditch and assigned every group of ten persons to dig forty cubits *(Ibn Kathir, Vol. III, p. 192)*. The length of the trench was about five thousand cubits; its depth varied between seven to ten cubits, and the width was normally nine cubits or a little more *(Ghazwah Ahzab by*

Examples of Great Muslims Who Had Creativity

Abu Bakr (RA)

"When the Muslims increased day by day, and the city of Madeenah had become filled with people wanting to embrace Islaam, the hostility also increased. Muslims of Makkah began preparing to migrate to Madeenah, as did Abu Bakr; however, the Prophet (PBUH) told him not to prepare or pack his bags, as he would be accompanying the Prophet when he received the command by Allaah, to migrate.

Overjoyed that he would have the honor of being the sole person to accompany Allaah's Messenger to Madeenah, he spent 4 months waiting for the command from Allaah, for Muhammad (PBUH) to migrate.

On this occasion, Aisha (RA) narrated that the Prophet used to visit her house in the morning and the evening. One day he came to her house at a time he never did before, and he had his face covered. As he entered the house, he said, *'If there is anybody else here, tell him to leave the place'.*

Abu Bakr replied that nobody else was present except his own family members. The Prophet then told them that he had received the orders for migration. Having had waited for this day for almost 4 months, he immediately began packing his bags for the journey. Aisha and Asma assisted in the packing. Asma could not find any

rope to knot some of the things together, so she tore her own cloth that was folded around her waist, and fastened the goods with it. Abu Bakr had already arranged 2 camels; one he offered to the Prophet, and he mounted the other himself. Thus in this way, the Prophet of Allaah and the *Siddeeq* began their journey to Madeenah."
(Sahih Bukhari)
(http://nelsonmuslims.co.uk/nmc_/content/view/145/39/)

What makes this situation creative is that Abu Bakr (RA) was preparing himself for a situation like this. He was creative in thinking about what they might need on this journey.

Khalid Bin Al-Waleed(RA)
A Military Genius

"It was two months after Khalid Bin Al-Waleed (RA) had embraced the religion of Islaam that he participated in his first battle; the Battle of Mu'tah. The Muslim army was only about 3,000 troops, many of whom were well known *Sahaabah*. They did not anticipate that they were about to face 100,000 Roman troops.

As the battle proceeded, the Muslim army lost the three commanders that had been appointed by the Prophet (PBUH). The Muslims overwhelmingly chose Khalid Bin Al-Waleed (RA) as the army commander.

Khalid (RA) took command and did what was best done in such a situation: safe retreat. His plan showed his tactical military brilliance. First he made the enemy believe that the Muslims were not planning on surrendering, but on attacking; and indeed the Muslim army withstood the opponent till nightfall. During the darkness of the night, Khalid (RA), with his brilliance, swapped the right division of the army with the left, and the left division with the right. He exchanged the rear battalions of the army with the front and vice versa. He then detached part of the army so that they could raise dust at the back of the Muslim troops and create commotion at sunrise.

At the time of sunrise, the Roman soldiers set eyes on new soldiers facing them, and the dust and noise were flooding the Muslim army; so they thought the Muslims had been receiving re-enforcements. Khalid (RA) then started his tactical retreat into the desert. The Romans did not follow the Muslims in their retreat in fear of a trap that was set for them in the barren desert.

That day Khalid Bin Al-Waleed (RA) was the last to retreat as he protected the backs of his soldiers and in doing so he broke 9 swords, fending off Roman attackers. When the Muslim army reached Madeenah, the people met them with accusations of fleeing the battle against the enemy, but the Prophet (PBUH), realizing that this was the best any commander could have done, declared the army as courageous faithful soldiers, who retreated to regroup and fight the enemy once again. Another *Sahaabah* who was creative and he was creative in the battle zone. This example shows that creativity comes in different ways."

(http://sahaba.net/modules.php?name=News&file=article&sid=60)

Umar ibn al-Khattab as a Khalifah

"Before his death, Abu Bakr (May Allaah be pleased with him) consulted the senior companions of the Prophet (Peace and Blessings of Allaah Be Upon Him) and nominated 'Umar (May Allaah be pleased with him) as the second Khalifah (leader) of the Muslims.

'Umar (RA) was the son of al-Khattab, and he is famous in Islaamic history as 'al-Farooq' (one who distinguishes between right and wrong). His acceptance of Islaam is notable.

'Umar (RA) was a brave and straightforward person. He was tough in his attitude and uncompromising in basic principles. He was a great and talented ruler. During his Caliphate, the frontiers of the Islaamic state expanded greatly.

'Umar (RA) was a strong administrator. He noticed the tremendous popularity of Khalid (RA), the Commander-in-Chief of the Muslim forces, and feared that the people might think too highly of him. So he removed Khalid (RA) and appointed Abu 'Ubaidah bin al-Jarrah (RA) as the Commander-in-Chief. The other reason for this bold decision was to make it clear that no one was indispensable and victory in war was actually due to Allaah's Help.

According to Shibli Nu'mani, the deposition of Khalid (RA) took place in 17 AH, after the conquest of Syria (ash-Sham). Some historians, however, maintain that this was the first command given by the Khalifah 'Umar (RA).

It takes a creative leader to think, who can be his successor, who would be a great leader in every way and run a Nation." *(http://bariisiyobasto.wordpress.com/2009/04/10/the-4-caliphs-of-islam-umar-ibn-al-khattab/)*

Story of a Muslim Child Who Used His Creativity

Kaiser Ahmed — Greenford, UK

Kaiser Ahmed is the 14-year-old chairman of "Quick-Learn Education"; a free, online learning service.

At 12, Ahmed had to start from scratch, having no money to invest in his company. Beginning with a vision and a solid business plan, he overcame many obstacles to get where he is today. In fact, just as Ahmed was putting the finishing touches on his website, preparing to launch his company, he fell victim to an online hacker, and lost everything he worked so hard to achieve. Not letting this incident deter him or his dreams, Ahmed started over. Rebuilding the website, ramping up advertising efforts, and enlisting the help of volunteers; his dream once again became a reality.

Today the site contains 22 lesson plans which help students who are 15 and under with a variety of topics they may have difficulties with in school. Ahmed's dedicated network of student volunteers help him create the lessons; which are approved by educators, and offer online student-to-student tutoring.

Kaiser Ahmed displays many of the qualities seen in great entrepreneurs. His determination, coupled with an extremely innovative and creative business sense has allowed him to reach his *goal. And at 14, he is confident that there is truly no limit to his potential. Learn more about his business at www.quicklearn.co.nr.*

Steps to Becoming Creative:

1. *Be curious, and look for different ways to do things.*
2. *Don't be afraid to be different.*
3. *Look at your mistakes as something to learn from.*
4. *Always learn new things.*
5. *Look for opportunities for you.*
6. *Learn from mentors.*
7. *Try to solve a problem.*
8. *Never be afraid to ask; you just don't know if they will say 'yes'.*

Activities

Write 5 things that you can be creative with. For example make a car, write a book, make a purse, teach in a different way, etc.

1. _____
_____

2. _____
_____

3. _____
_____

4. _____
_____

5. _____
_____

Imagination
-Anonymous

Open the doors
Of creativity
Let it all flow out
Take away
The barriers
To being who you are
Add some
Of your thoughts
And your sparks
You've got
Imagination
Use it all, have some fun
Kick back for a while
Don't work
Enjoy yourself
Have the time of your life
You can be
Whatever you want
You can go
Wherever you wish
There is no boundary
To where your imagination
Will lead

There is no stopping the fun
That you get to have
If you use your creativity
If you use your brain
Just go ride
The train of imagination.

Author's Biography

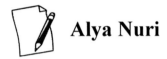 **Alya Nuri**

Alya Nuri, a 9-year old child author and speaker, started her writing career at the tender age of 7 and has now finally gotten her series, "Things Every Kid Should Know" on Smoking, Alcohol and Drugs published and available to purchase.

She loves reading books and working for the welfare of the poor and needy. She has written three articles and wants to continue writing more books for the betterment of the youth.

She wants to pursue her passion of public speaking and coaching kids. Currently she is co-authoring book number 4, and working on book number 5.

Have You Booked "The Most Inspirational Muslim Woman Speaker In America"?

Zohra Sarwari

The Ideal Professional Speaker for Your Next Event!

"Zohra Sarwari has a great skill for making you want to achieve on a higher level. Your students will enjoy learning from her!"

Jonathan Sprinkles
Former APCA National College 'Speaker of the Year'
www.jsprinkles.com

"After hearing Zohra Sarwari's speech, I was profoundly moved by her enthusiasm to further educate me on the way the Muslims live. Her knowledge instilled a greater understanding and appreciation in me."

Debbie Burke
High School Teacher
Indianapolis, Indiana

Interested in other products by Zohra? Take a look at what she has to offer:

'9 Steps To Achieve Your Destiny'
Do your best and let the Creator take care of the rest!

'9 Steps To Achieve Your Destiny' *explores the steps that, if practiced daily, will help you achieve your destiny-InshAllaah. It shows you how your thinking and habits can either make you successful or stagnant, and helps you navigate your way to the right choices and productive habits.*

How To Raise A Successful
KIDPRENEUR
Million Dollar Ideas For Kids

*Ever wondered why some kids had it all, while others didn't? Ever wondered how some parents taught great skills to their kids, while other's wish they could? Ever wondered how a kid could be a millionaire while there were millions of adults who couldn't? What is it that these kids have? Well you don't have to wonder anymore. Here is a book that does just that. In this book you will discover **'How to raise a successful kidprenuer'**, no matter who you are. All you need is this book and your determination. This book has all of the resources, and step by step plan outlined for you. If you're ready to take your child to the next level, and want advice from a mom who has been there and done that, then this book is for you!*

'Imagine that Today is Your Last Day'
How would you act if you knew that today was the last day of your life?

'Imagine that Today is Your Last Day' *reveals to you the secrets of living a great life and accepting your fate when it arrives. The book discusses the missing link in your life for which you will have to pay a price after death. Bring every moment to life, it can be your LAST day TODAY! It is an experience that many never think about, let alone go through it.*

NO! I AM NOT A TERRORIST!

'Terrorism' and 'terrorist' are the latest media buzzwords! However, do you actually know what each of these terms mean? Do you know who a 'terrorist' is? What comes to your mind when you think of a 'terrorist'? Is it a man with a beard, or is it a woman in a veil? Muslims worldwide are being stereotyped and labeled as 'terrorists'. Have you ever stopped and wondered why? Have you ever made the time to discover what lies under the beard and the dress? Have you ever stopped to think what Islaam actually has to say about 'terrorism'? Find the answers to all the above questions and more in this book, **'NO! I AM NOT A TERRORIST!'**

Are Muslim Women Oppressed?
Beyond the Veil

ZOHRA SARWARI

Learn about the dignified and well-managed lives of Muslim women and know the reasons why they dress the way they do. **'Are Muslim Women OPPRESSED?'** *answers your questions: Why do Muslim women wear those weird clothes? Are they doing it for men? Are they inferior? Do they have no rights*? **'Are Muslim Women OPPRESSED?'** *will reveal the truth behind the concealed Muslim woman. It is a voyage from behind the veil to the real freedom and will give you an insight about Muslim women like you have never read before. Read and clear the misconceptions; separate the facts from the* myths!

Powerful Time Management Skills for Muslims

Islaam holds Muslims responsible for every action they do and they will be held answerable for the things they are blessed with and how they used it. One of these blessings is 'Time'. **Powerful Time Management Skills for Muslims** *is explaining using references from the Qur'aan and Sunnah how Muslims should live their lives and utilize the precious gift of 'Time'.*

Speaking Skills Every Muslim Must Know

Confidence is the key to success. **Speaking Skills Every Muslim Must Know** *shares with you some vital methods and techniques to develop confidence and helps you overcome your fear of public speaking. The book guides you following the pattern applied by the Prophet Muhammad (PBUH) and how he delivered his speeches.*

Who Am I?
Figure Out YOUR Identity

Have you ever wondered who you are? Do you know your strengths and weaknesses? Have you ever wondered who you don't want to be? Have you tried to fit in but couldn't find the right place? **'Who Am I'** *is a book that identifies who a Muslim teen is and what characteristics one should possess. It defines who you are and who you want to become.* **'Who Am I?'** *will take you on a journey that will help you not only discover who you really are, but also strengthen your skills in leadership, time-management and self-esteem insha'Allaah.*

Time Management for Success
(e-book)

Become a Professional Speaker Today
(e-book)

Special Quantity Discount Offer!

- ► 20-99 books $12.00 per copy
- ► 100-499 books $9.00 each
- ► 500-999 books $7.00 each

Have You Bought The Series "Things Every Kid Should Know: Smoking, Drugs and Alcohol" for Your Kids?

Written By A
"9 Year Old" Muslim Author,
Alya Nuri

Things Every Kid Should Know - Drugs!

'Things Every Kid Should Know - Drugs!' *will walk you through what Drugs are; why they are bad for you, and how to avoid picking up this bad habit. There is a story of a young man who goes through his high school doing drugs, and what happens in his life due to making that choice. There are also facts in the story to help understand the issue of Drugs.*

Things Every Kid Should Know - Alcohol!

'Things Every Kid Should Know - Alcohol!' *will walk you through what Alcohol is; why it is bad for you, and how to avoid picking up this bad habit. There is a story of a girl who discovers Alcohol at a friend's house. Her curiosity makes her want to learn more about the topic, but when her friend's dad gets into trouble because of it, she makes a vow. There are also facts in the story to help understand the issues relating to Alcohol.*

Things Every Kid Should Know - Smoking!

'Things Every Kid Should Know - Smoking!' *will walk you through what Smoking is; why it is bad for you, and how to avoid picking up this bad habit. There is a story of two young friends who go through life, and what happens along their lives as they each make different choices. There are also facts in the story to help understand all the issues relating to Smoking.*

Breinigsville, PA USA
05 November 2009
227122BV00001B/2/P